I0473776

GET THE JOB

by Brian Bigelow

Get The Job
by Brian Bigelow
ISBN: 13: 978-1467996129
ISBN: 10: 1467996122

Dedication

This book is dedicated to my wife Brandy who stood beside me and supported me through the many job hunts. She really helped with deal with the stress that I've had when I was between jobs.

After seeing the difficulty my two Sons were having in finding jobs also was part of the impetus for this book. Therefore it is also dedicated to Charlie and Joey and their finding their way in this world.

This book is also dedicated to helping the many that are hunting for jobs out there presently. May every one of you be successful in your search.

"Watch your thoughts,
for they become words.
Watch your words,
for they become actions.
Watch your actions,
for they become habits.
Watch your habits,
for they become character.
Watch your character,
for it becomes your destiny."

Lao Tze

"You cannot have the success without the failures."

Blondie Hasler American Yachtsman

Contents

About the author

Having done a lot of job searching in a fairly short time brings with it a lot of experience. This book mostly focuses on the years since 2005 when I was laid off from a truck stop in Fountain, Colorado. They required me to finally use the paid time off that I had accumulated and when it came time to go back to work I no longer had a job. That's when I began collecting unemployment for the next six months until it ran out. We ended up losing the mobile home that we were living in since I had no income any longer to pay the mortgage or lot rent. Shortly after this my wife and I had to live in an extremely small Toyota as I recall for a while. I can't say that this was the best time of my life especially after the car broke and we ended up staying in a shelter and then at a friends house for a short time.

Since then I have worked in apartment maintenance, call centers and presently I'm working in retail. I've also had to find all of those changes during the worst economic downturn since the 1930's. I'll go into detail some of the experiences that I had when I decided that I had to get us off of the streets. These experiences really changed me in so many ways and I can truly say that I completely changed the course of my life. Of course, I think it would cause anyone to have a major change in the direction that they are headed. Because of what I went through I do feel that I have a few things to share with everyone that most of the people that write these type of books doesn't. I've really been where I feel is the bottom, I've never been back and I never will.

Introduction

No matter what you are dealing with at present it's really not that bad, believe me you'll make it through this time in your life. From this point forward you have so many roads that you can travel on to the future that awaits you. You have so many choices that are available to you right now at this point in your life. Really, when you think about it there are a lot of options that are open to you. You can either work in a field that you know well or you can also make a real change to something radically different. This is something that I did and I really changed the course of my life. It all comes down to how you market yourself and hunting for a job definitely involves marketing these days and actually has for many years.

In this book I have included many tips that are available for you to try regardless of what your choice is on where you want to work. I've also included a few things that weren't very successful for finding employment for myself and for a few others. Also, I've included many very successful techniques of which most of them I've tried at some point. Personally, the best way to learn is from the mistakes that someone else has made and I've made a few of them over the years. Actually, I'm not sure that they were really mistakes as I did learn from each attempt that I made. Therefore those attempts are something that I do consider to be learning experiences.

I'll admit that at one time I found hunting for a job to be one of the most stressful things that I could possibly do with my time. Interviews in particular are something that I found to be extremely stressful experiences that scared me a lot. What I learned is that they don't have to be all that scary in reality if you are properly prepared. Even at first trying to write a resume was something that was a bit scary for me as a resume helps you get an interview. This was because I didn't know how to write an effective resume back then. That all changed because I studied carefully to learn how to be more effective in searching for a job as I would rather be working then not working. It was quite the learning experience that I gained a lot from and of course the ability to earn a paycheck.

When you look through the news, the blogs, the social networking sites it's easy to find stories about people that have been looking for employment for a long time. In most cases if they were more effectively marketing themselves they would be employed and no longer have to be searching for a job. They are not the focus of this book, finding your next job so that you can start to earn a living is. Through these pages you'll learn how to get your application or resume at the top of the stack so that yours will be selected. You'll learn how to effectively market yourself so that you can get the job and begin earning a paycheck again. This is something that I felt I could do something about, that I could help with since I have been there myself.

Never regret.
If it's good,
it's wonderful.
If it's bad,
it's experience.
Victoria Holt

Find A Need

This is the place that I was at in 2005 after working at a truck stop for 3 years and numerous other times that have came before and after. Always I had to ask the same exact question every time which is where do I begin to go from here. This has been a rather appropriate question for me just as it is for you to ask as you will soon see later in this chapter. Each time I would come up with a plan that would help guide me along the way from that place in my life. If I hadn't been able to have a plan in place I knew that I wouldn't get very far.

My job searches had always been relatively easy until late in 2007 after I had lost my job at Hewlett Packard on the USPS help desk. It really hadn't ever been too difficult for me to find jobs in many different places over the years. I can truly say that it wasn't difficult to be a "jack of all trades and a master of none." At one time I was a carpenter's helper on a framing crew when I was building houses. There were even times that I did hot tar roofing, shingled roofing, hauled concrete forms, painting houses and some plastering.

In between various construction gigs I also moved household goods and packed up entire households for many years on and off. Mostly working in the moving industry was a summer job only for me. During the winter the moving industry slows down and then I felt it would be time for me make another change and find a another job. Needless to say that I worked at a lot of different jobs over the years as I didn't have a true lifelong career being that I was a true opportunist. Still, each time the question always came up which is where do I begin to go from here.

When I think of changing jobs it's a bit like being at a crossroads for me every time. From the point that I am at

4

there are at least two roads (and usually more) that are leading off into the distance. So for me there are always many choices available for my future paths just as there is for you. It all really depends on where you really want to go, just because you've been following a specific path doesn't mean you have to stay on that path. You can change your course in life even if it is somewhat more difficult than it used to be.

To make the change and decide on a course I would have to decide what I wanted to do with my life. This was at least for the time being only for me since it was never a permanent thing. Once I decided what I wanted to do I then researched it as thoroughly as I could. I found out what the employers in my new chosen field was looking for and then I would do my best to match that. That has always applied and it always will regardless of the job market.

"Find a need and fill it"-Ruth Stafford Peale, wife of Norman Vincent Peale.

Throughout growing up with my grandparents that quote I heard many times from my grandfather. Employers have specific needs in mind when they are looking for a new employee. This is something that definitely requires research into what that just might be which is much easier than it used to be because of the internet. So much information about companies is easily available these days within minutes. Still you have to do some legwork and actually meet with people to get the most useful information. You can't just count on the internet alone to provide you with all of the information that you need to find the need to fill.

If you are going to be working with customers on a regular basis you need communication skills and the correct personality. Repairing computers also has a specific set of technical requirements that very few other occupations will use or need. Building houses requires a knowledge of tools, safety and how things goes together. Moving furniture requires you to be able to move things quickly without hurting yourself. These are all jobs that I have had at various times in all of years that I have been working and all of them require a very specific skillet and each has job also has it's own specific set of needs.

A couple of good sites to find out company information and what they need are at these sites:

Glass Door: http://www.glassdoor.com/

Linked In: http://www.linkedin.com/

Manta: http://www.manta.com/

While these are great sites to get information from that you need to know be aware ahead of time that you might find a lot of negative information especially on Glass Door. Don't pass up any opportunities to talk with employees at the companies you are interested in working for. They are sometimes the best sources for the information that you really need, you can even get great interview and application/resume pointers. That way you will be more successful when you do apply because you'll be able to cut to the chase and offer what that employer needs. What you are looking for is especially the things that outside of the ordinary that wouldn't be asked in the average interview. So you need to be prepared to really probe with your questions, you might also need to buy the employee or business owner a cup of coffee or a soft drink.

Having done some research with actual employees and business owners I wouldn't recommend offering most donuts or other sweets. Just about every one did seem to like their coffee though so that would be a great thing to offer just about everyone you talk to. For those that don't drink coffee though you need to be ready to offer a soft drink instead. I remember reading about someone that would bring around a thermos and paper cups with them while they were networking. From what I can remember that was rather successful. Come to think it was tried at one of the call centers that I worked at by someone that interested in joining the company. Because of the initial offering they became personal friends with the manager they had talked to in the parking lot who gave them a personal recommendation when that person lost their job at the call center.

What I'm trying to get at here is you can't just rely only on the information that you will find at company employment websites. Though there is a lot of information on those sites you won't find out everything that you need to know. Sometimes there are specific things that you won't get from the website. One right off the top of my head is Walmart, apparently you need to show during an interview a time where you were taking charge. Apparently, you could also state during an interview a time when a fellow employee recommended that you should become a leader, supervisor, etc. There was an individual that I spent about 20 minutes with that had worked for Walmart three months at the time that I talked to him and I got a lot of information from him. I had been wondering why I was not successful in getting a job at Walmart previously while beginning my research for this book.

From that example you might need take some time to find out what you need to know and you probably will need to ask some good probing questions. There is no way that I could cover what every last employer is needing in this book. I would probably need several thousand pages more than I will have written because every employer is different in what they are looking for and what they need.

Optimism Counts

Optimism is a trait that is simply when someone is expecting the best possible outcome from the situation that they happen to be in. This is a very necessary quality to have when you are out hunting for a job and always has been. You really do need a positive outlook as it will help keep you wanting to continue the search that you're now embarked upon. Without optimism on your side you may not possibly want to continue the search. This will also help you in your ability to sound enthusiastic when you are in an interview.

While it is difficult to maintain an optimistic attitude throughout your job hunt it is really a necessity. This I can state from personal experience as I have had to do a lot of job hunting over the years. Each morning when I was between jobs I would wake up and then sit at the edge of the bed. After doing so I would tell myself that I was going to be successful that day. Also after I got out of bed I would stand in front of the mirror and tell myself to be positive, that I would be optimistic that day.

This was especially necessary for me because every time I would read the news I found it to be rather depressing. So many people were out of work for a long time and also I'll admit that my resume response wasn't too high at one time either. Of course, the way that I wrote my resume was a big contributor to my poor resume response rate. At the time I didn't realize that, I just thought that a lot of employers either weren't hiring or that they just weren't interested in me. It was something that I had let affect my outlook on life in general. It also didn't go so well when there was a phone interview or when I was attempting to network because of my attitude.

When you are optimistic it affects the way that you

interact with others, especially whenever you are in an interview. As my Grandmother used to say "you attract more flies with honey than with vinegar". While that old saying sounds rather quaint and folksy it applies the entire time that you are searching for a job. If you sound positive it projects so much better, you leave a much better impression on others. This is especially true of first impressions of the decision makers when it comes to hiring you.

Sounding optimistic is a bit like an acting skill for many people, it really was for me at one time. I'll admit that at one time I was an extremely negative person, very unpleasant to be around. You wouldn't have thought of me as the life of party and I can't say that I had any friends. As time went on it became easier and easier for me to at least act optimistic when I needed to because of practicing. Now I really am a bit optimistic most of the time and I show it, sometimes you could even call me charming now.

By being optimistic you will increase your chances of getting calls for interviews. You will also increase your success rate at interviews which definitely isn't a bad thing. After you have been successful at an interview and gotten a job you will also be able stay employed longer. This will also allow you to have better interpersonal relationships with the people you work with on a daily basis.

A pessimist sees the difficulty in every opportunity;
an optimist sees he opportunity in every difficulty
Winston Churchill

Enthusiasm Pays

I don't think you lead by pessimism and cynicism.
I think you lead by optimism and enthusiasm and energy .
Patricia Ireland

In the last chapter I discussed optimism which is a very important trait to have during any job hunt. While optimism is an internal trait that helps you to see things positively that are around you, enthusiasm is more external. It's what others see as an outgrow of what is within you. When you are showing others the optimism that is within you it is usually seen as enthusiasm. This is something you really want to demonstrate during an interview as most employers are looking for it. They want to hire someone that sounds happy and shows that they want to be there. This is one attribute that will definitely increase your chances of success during interviews.

Think about it for a moment, about the times that you go to the store to do a little shopping. Which kind of clerk or salesperson would you rather see, one that displays a quiet enthusiasm or one that doesn't seem too happy? You are probably just like me in preferring to meet the clerk or salesperson that shows enthusiasm over one that doesn't. Well, this applies to the people that are conducting interviews also. Most interviewers will hire someone that is enthusiastic over someone that isn't if the two people have the exact same qualifications.

What I mean by showing enthusiasm is someone that sounds like they want to be there, that has a positive outlook on life. This is always attractive to people and draws them in. They want to be around you, to have you near them which is definitely in your favor when you are hunting for a job. We're not talking about trying be someone that is over the top like the pitchmen that do those TV sales commercials. You know the ones I'm talking about, they are so annoying. Those pitchmen are so enthusiastic that they are to the point that they are so excited.

We're talking about being someone that is quietly enthusiastic. You demonstrate that you want to be there by your expressions, your tone and your body language. It's amazing how much someone can read about you from your body language alone. You want your speech and body language to match each other, if they don't you probably won't get the job. These both need to show enthusiasm at the same time. Considering how I used to act, if I can do it I know for sure that you will be able to.

Self Confidence

*Being on stage is
about self esteem
and self confidence.
Jake Miller*

A job hunt can seem to be such an overwhelming process these days and it can also take a really long time for anyone. Optimism and enthusiasm can keep you going, in fact they are a major part of what becomes self confidence in an individual. You need to know and believe that you will succeed before you get out of bed and go out of the door each day. You need to realize that you are the answer to a need that an employer has and the solution they are looking for. Knowing this is important because no one has exactly what you have to offer an employer. Being self confident is an attribute that is of an absolute necessity for any job market, especially these last few years.

Without self-confidence you will not succeed in getting a job anywhere in the world at any time except by luck alone. This is something that I firmly believe and has become a driving force for me in my various job searches. It is something that has always proven true throughout history. Successful people have always been self-confident, they believe in their innate abilities. Therefore, the take-away is that you need self confidence everyday in your abilities also so that you can be successful in what you are doing. This is something that doesn't just apply to your present job hunt, it applies to your entire life.

So the question is how do you become self confident? What I had to do to start becoming self-confident was to tell myself each day that I would be successful. These self affirmations helped me to begin to direct my outlook on life and my job search each day. After a while I began to believe it and made it a part of my permanent way of thinking. I also began seeing myself working in the job that I was applying or interviewing for. This gave me a target to begin shooting for. Practicing my interview skills also helped a lot in the building of my self confidence. Nothing else can build self confidence quite as much as being prepared for what you know will be coming.

Writing this book required self-confidence on my part come to think of it. I had to be confident in my ability to communicate ideas effectively to the average person. It has allowed me to continue and has drove me to continue to write as this book has taken shape. Not only has it helped me to continue to write but it has also helped me to finish each chapter and the entire book. It in fact is somewhat the same as having the self confidence that's required for a successful job search.

Self confidence begins form within the mind so therefore it is created within your thought processes. By thinking it, you will become self confident and it becomes part of you and it affects your outlook. This is something that I realized quite a few years ago. You also need to realize it and make it a part of your entire being. A self confident individual will always succeed where someone else will fail. They know that they will be successful before they ever start. This is because the believe strongly in their abilities and what they have to offer.

During an interview, self confidence is an important part of the decision that will be made on you being hired. It requires you to demonstrate that self-confidence that is with in you. A self confident individual shows a can do attitude, that they can accomplish the tasks that are set before them. This quality in life is always an attractive quality, it draws people in, especially hiring decision makers. Also, it will help you to keep a job longer once you have found a job again.

We are what we think.
All that we are arises
with our thoughts.
With our thoughts,
we make our world.
Buddha

Notice that he is stating that we make our own world by our thoughts. Our thoughts are what guides actions throughout our lives so that one thing is always true.

What we think,
we become.
Buddha

Be Proactive

As soon as I became proactive
in producing my own stuff,
I started getting other roles.
Ray Liotta

Regardless of what job you are going for you need to be proactive in your job hunt. I really can't stress this enough, you need to act on every possible opportunity that comes up. At times you even need to create the opportunity and go knocking on a few doors. While you can post your resume on all of the job search sites and engines it might not get you any calls. Also, you may be waiting a long time if you continue to wait for the call from the hiring manager that now has the ultimate position ready for you. You sometimes need to be very proactive and be prepared to act on your own.

      Probably the most proactive that I've ever been was when I decided that I wanted to work in apartment maintenance. How I decided that I wanted to proceed with this was to cold call every apartment complex in the city. As I recall I decided the question that would ask would be "what positions are you hiring for" after a few of the calls. Though I had asked "are you hiring" for the first few calls I soon decided that it was not presumptive enough for what I was doing, I was looking for a definite opening somewhere. It really didn't interest me to fill out applications for several days and not hear anything from most of them.

      In a quiet part of the house I practiced my phone etiquette and questions several times out loud before starting to make any of the calls. My wife was looking at me a bit strangely a couple of times when she noticed this, I had to explain what I was doing. After my practicing a number of times I opened the phone book and proceeded to call every apartment complex listed from A to Z, it was just under 200 apartment complexes. From this effort I had managed to get interviews at two different apartment complexes.

Since I was expecting a high rate of no's before making my calls I prepared myself so that I wouldn't be taking it personally. After all, they weren't expecting a call from me. Still, about halfway through the phone book it did get to me a bit so I had to take a little break so that I could prepare myself to make the calls again. It was a good thing that I did that because after I returned to the phone is when I managed to get the interviews set up. For each positive response I had a notebook open, ready to write down any pertinent information like who I would be seeing and what time.

After getting the two interviews set up I mapped them out carefully as I needed to know for sure where I was going. I made sure that I got to each apartment complex about 20 minutes before the agreed to time, that way I could get into the office itself 10 minutes before. The second apartment complex hired me right then on a contingency basis. This shows what being proactive in your job hunt can do for you.

When you are cold calling like I was you need to sound very, very positive with every call. It can be a very successful technique that can shorten your job hunt by several weeks. At the same time it is extremely stressful because of all the no answers you will receive so be prepared. What helped me to continue with the calls was thinking of all the telemarketers and collection agents over the years that had called me (yes, I used to have a lot of bad debts at one time). I'm sure that they received no's during most of the calls that they made but it didn't stop them and you can't let it stop you so always be proactive in your job hunt.

Taking A Break

*"If you truly seek understanding,
then first, empty your cup!"*
Buddhist quote

Occasionally it is actually necessary to take a little break from a job hunt, you just don't want to take too long of a break. After spending several hours at a time hitting the pavement networking and submitting applications and resumes I found that taking a break was necessary. Sometimes this would involve going down to a nearby lake to feed the ducks and geese and allow my mind to wander a bit and become clear again. There were other times that I would stop by a stream and listen to the sounds of the moving water as I allowed myself to become immersed in them. Another one of my favorites for taking a break is to listen to wind sounds as it goes through the trees. I've even found that watching the clouds for a little bit has been very useful in eliminating the stress. None of these things take very long but they are all extremely effective.

It is necessary for your sanity to get away from the job hunt just for a little bit now and then. Job hunts can be, and I have found them to be, often quite stressful for me in the past. Taking a little break helps to refresh your mind and your focus on what you'll need to do later in the day. Many times also while taking a little break a solution will present itself to you once you are no longer focused directly on the problem at hand. This could be one of the sentences in your resume that you were wanting to say exactly the right thing while you are going through a complete rewrite. For an effective resume it really takes time and focus to write well but there is such a thing as overdoing it.

Another time for clearing my mind would be while waiting in the office for an interview to begin. One of the things that I learned from Buddhism is a simple meditation technique. You close your eyes, focus on your breathing while taking deep breaths and then you begin to empty your mind. While you probably won't be able to completely empty your mind the first couple of times you try it you probably will on subsequent times. With your mind now emptied and cleared of all of the clutter you will be able to more easily focus clearly on what you need to do.

Many years ago there an artist called Georges Seurat who painted entire paintings with little dots of paint. He started an entire movement of painting with dots Probably the most famous is one where there are a number of people having a picnic on a lakeshore and you can see some boats in the distance. It's called "A Sunday on La Grande". Because it is made up of little dots if you are real close the painting wouldn't make any sense, by standing back a bit the picture becomes clear. This is what taking a little break every now and then does for you, it allows you to see clearly again what you need to. It allows you to reach a true understanding and to be more successful in everything that you do including any job search that you are on.

Acting Skills

All the world's a stage,
And all the men and women merely players;
They have their exits and entrances,
And one man in has time plays many parts...
William Shakespeare
from As You Like It

One of the most useful techniques that I've used in preparation has been to interview myself in front of a mirror. This allowed me to see myself from an interviewers point of view. I could readily see where my body language didn't match what I was saying during the interview. I could also see my hands moving around and my knee or foot jerking as I was very nervous and still am to this day. For the first time I could really see the way that I was acting and knew what it looked like. I know that I probably wouldn't hire someone now that fidgeted like I did back then.

I had to teach myself how to be still because someone that is figiting doesn't look like they are paying close attention. It didn't take long to learn to force my hands to stay still upon my knees and to force my knees to quit moving, jerking up and down. Also I forced myself to look directly at my reflection in the eye. Eye contact reinforces to the interviewer that you are listening to them and them alone, that you are focusing on them. Body language is an important part of acting skills that are necessary during an interview. Without them you will not be successful at gaining a new job I can guarantee anyone. This is something that I personally experienced in my own life.

My recommendation to anyone that is hunting for a job is that they pay attention to their posture both when sitting and standing. Slouching in a chair shows someone that the individual slouching is lazy, that is actually the image in most peoples minds. This in particular applies to those that conduct interviews. They see so many people for a position these days that the way someone is sitting could easily be a deciding factor in whether they hire them or not. While this is unfortunate for many that are looking for a job it still is a fact presently and will be for a while yet. You always have to keep in mind that appearances always matter and so do first impressions. In about 20 seconds in most cases the interviewer has already made up their mind and you really don't get a second chance.

Just because someone hasn't been successful in interviews in the past doesn't mean that things can't change. By learning to control your body language you can definitely improve your interview skills and increase your chances of being hired. I know this one for a fact as I have been very successful in looking for and finding jobs during the worst employment downturn since the Great Depression. You really don't have to be unemployed if you don't want to, you just have to take control of the situation and not let it control you. Your body language and the way you act are things that you can control if you want to. It just takes being able to be open to observing yourself and the way that you are acting and then change what doesn't make a good impression to others.

If we don't change,
we don't grow.
If we don't grow,
we aren't really living
Gail Sheehy

By making changes to the way you act you begin to grow, to

become a different person. At least you will be a different person in the eyes of a future interviewer or a decision maker that you meet. Remember, you really do need to impress the interviewer immediately, within the first few seconds at a minimum. Developing those acting skills for interviews will help you with that from the first moment you are in an interview.

What to offer

It is our attitude at the beginning of a difficult task which, more than anything else, will affect it's successful outcome.
William James

Beyond what I've already covered in previous chapters of this book you need to show that you are a motivated individual. You need to bring together your enthusiasm, the research you've conducted and your skill set to that company. By being knowledgeable about what they are looking you are showing that you are motivated. You need to show that will be able to get the job done that they will be hiring you for, that you are motivated to do that job. When it comes to a business you need to be motivated to do what they need to succeed. This is not something that is all about you when you are hunting for a job, it's all about what the employer needs at least during the hiring process. Once you are hired then it becomes what they will be doing for you like your paycheck, benefits, work/life balance, etc.

  First of all you need to show that you are motivated to be there at the interview, that you want to be there. While I'm not sure that bubbly excitement is what you need to show you do need to speak positively and have a positive tone to your voice. In moments they will be able to tell if you don't want to be there really as I know from personal experience. Eye contact helps to reinforce showing the interviewer that you have the motivation that you are attempting to show during the interview. I'm not talking about staring them down, I'm talking about glances where you look them in the eye each time. This is something that I used to have a problem with as I couldn't look anyone in the eye directly at one time. I was really quite the introvert, didn't really like speaking to anyone face to face. I had to teach myself how to put my interview acting skills to use in order to make sure that I could take care of my family.

That all being said there are some jobs where you do need to show what motivates you to some extant. In call centers and retail jobs you need to show that taking care of the customer first and foremost is one of the things motivates you. Sales positions require you to be motivated by high earnings most of all, in some ways it pays to be greedy. Technical positions like computer repair have the requirement of needing to gain more technical knowledge as a motivating factor. Accountants are quite often motivated by accuracy most of all. While all of these positions require you to show what personally motivates you they are all motivations that are specifically work related.

This all comes back to offering specifically to filling a need that an employer has. To go into a little further detail I've made a few career changes over the years, some of those have been big changes. At one time I worked in a truck stop, began as a janitor at the store and fuel desk and later I was promoted to cashier. When I changed careers to working in call centers do you think I called attention to the fact that I had to clean the store on a daily basis? What I called attention to was my experience with the customers and communicating with my coworkers every day that I was at work. Cleaning the store did not apply to the call center positions so I didn't mention it during an interview.

No matter what your experience happens to be only demonstrate that you have what an employer is looking for, this is what you offer. Nothing else and nothing more. By offering specifically what the employer is looking for you will increase your chances exponentially for getting the job.

Networking

It's all about people.
It's about networking
and being nice to people
and not burning any bridges.
Your book is going to impress,
but in the end it is people
that are going to hire you

Mike Davidson

A good definition of networking is meeting people to build relationships for employment or business purposes. There is two main forms of networking that occurs, one is online social networking and there is face to face networking where are meeting people. We'll first consider online social networking in this chapter and then later face to face networking. Social networking is something that has become a big part of a lot of peoples lives these days. I personally do have Twitter, Facebook, Linked In, Google+ and MySpace accounts of which I access Facebook daily and the others not quite so often. I really enjoy some of the feeds and postings that I get, some of them are quite interesting especially on Facebook.

Twitter: www.twitter.com

Facebook: www.facebook.com

Linked In: www.inkedin.com

MySpace: www.myspace.com

Presently, at the time of writing this book Google+ is by invitation only but since it won't be at some point: plus.google.com/

Most of these social networking sites have one thing in common, you can waste a lot of time on them and not get any closer to getting a job. You won't even get any good job hunting tips on most of these sites unless you dig a little deeper. On Facebook there are a number of pages that are pretty good that have some really good information like mine "Get the Job" which is what I named this book for. (Just had to toot my own horn a little there). There are even a couple of good job search applications like "Branch Out" and "Be Known" now on Facebook. "Branch Out" has a built in "Indeed" job search engine and "Be Known" has a built in "Monster" job search engine. Both of them seems to work pretty well from my experience with having tried them out. They seem to be doing a good job of filling a need that has existed in social networking as a whole in my opinion.

Be Known: apps.facebook.com/beknown/

Branch Out: apps.facebook.com/branchout/

Probably the best one of all the social networking sites in my opinion for finding job hunting information is Linked In. Once you connect with the job coaches on Linked In you will receive a lot of very useful information and tips on a daily basis. I've also used the job search engine which didn't seem to have a lot of positions posted for where I live at but you can check it out. In fact I recommend checking it out, they do seem to have a lot of postings that you won't find anywhere else online. You just might find the opportunity of a lifetime after spending just a few minutes of your time, you never know.

Also what I've done on Linked In is research what companies are looking for in a new employee at their company. Most of the hiring decision makers at quite a few companies have Linked In accounts which they do access rather regularly even if not every day. If you do contact one of the decision makers don't expect an immediate response, sometimes it has been several days for me to receive an answer. In quite a few cases I've received no response whatsoever from the person I messaged. While this is something that I found a bit frustrating many who are on Linked In will not respond to someone that they don't personally know.

While I have read about finding jobs through Twitter I personally haven't had any luck there when I tried there. Most of the successful people have been in advertising and marketing which has some great opportunities available as companies are trying to gain new customers. More recently I've read about, though I haven't exactly seen it on my feeds, some companies have been posting openings on Twitter only. A search engine only for Twitter that just started recently which opens some interesting possibilities is Twit Job search at twitjobsearch.com/

In the search window underneath "What do you want to do?" you need to type in the job title and at a minimum the state. The search engine loads really quickly on a real time basis and it will keep loading for a while as it keeps searching for posted openings. Make sure you refine by clicking your town on the right otherwise it will include openings from the entire state you are in. Sometimes you will see nationwide postings that will still come up. My next job hunt this search engine will be one of my primary ones I can tell already.

Enough of social networking for now, let's move on to

face to face networking. It actually is probably the most important method in the present job market and probably half of all jobs are found through face to face networking. I've read many articles where job seekers never bothered with searching on the internet more recently. They just started networking, meeting people and doing the legwork which is the way you used to have to do it. Even today I don't think I'll ever forget going door to door to each business networking though I didn't call it that in those days. It was just part of the job hunt for me and for so many others back then in the early to mid 80's, in some ways we've almost come full circle.

The most important trip you may take
in life is meeting people halfway.
Henry Boye

The legwork is necessary these days, get out from behind the computer and start meeting some people. If you are only searching for a job through the internet you've eliminated many of the possibilities and opportunities for you. From what I understand that only about 10%-20% of all jobs are posted online though I really think that it's a bit higher than those numbers. Still, even if it's 50%-75% of all openings are posted online then you're missing out on a lot of opportunities if you don't face to face network. Many job coaches that I read postings from call this part of the hidden job market, these openings that aren't posted online.

You don't need to wear a three piece suit to network as a rule unless you are attempting to network at a banking or lawyers convention and other similar venues. However, since first impressions do matter you do need to dress up a bit for effective networking. It could very well be that the next person you meet will offer you the opportunity of a lifetime because of their impressions of you. So, make the most of the moment by making the best first impression you can. Of course, you could also find out about that great opportunity that a neighbor or friend knows about at the company they work for. You can also find out what you need to know regarding what a company is really looking for because each company is different.

To help you to find out what companies are really looking for make sure you ask people questions that just got a job at one of your target companies. They are probably your best source for the information that you really need to get a job at that company. Usually the companies employment website will have rather limited information, quite often it is rather general in nature. They don't include everything on the website that you need to get a job there. Mainly, for the best results during networking you need to be as interesting as possible. You are wanting to get noticed more than anything.

Elevator Speeches

*Many of life's failures are people who did not realize
how close they were to success when they gave up.*
Thomas Edison

There is a lot of advice that you can find online about elevator speeches and the importance of having one during a job search. It has been especially suggested is having an elevator speech ready for when you are attending a job fair. They are simply a short one to three minute statement that says what you do and what you bring to an employer. While this originally was said in the short time it would normally take an elevator to from the top floor to the first floor. In most cases I suggest that the speech is even shorter. For me I ended up turning my elevator speech into my closing statement during interviews and it was about 20 seconds long.

I did attempt to use an elevator speech a few times at some job fairs but ended up not being able to use it. It seemed to me that there were too many job hunters all around me at the event. Also, because there was so many job hunters it was rather noisy so I wouldn't have been heard very well I felt. Along with that I was still pretty introverted which makes public speaking of any kind very difficult. This was after I practiced my little speech again and again many times. But since I don't like not using something that I work very hard on I had to find another use, so I turned it into my closing statement for interviews.

For me, my elevator speech which I turned into a closing statement went like this for call centers: "I would like to bring my extensive customer service experience, my ability to learn new software and always being on time to benefit the team. I'm so glad I got to have met you (name) today and look forward to hearing from you soon. Thank you so much for seeing me today!" Usually I would start to get up from my chair prepared to shake their hand just before heading out the door.

Since this was the very last opportunity for me to sell myself to the interviewer I did my best to make the moment count. There was more than once it was a very effective addition to my interview methods since I put my first elevator speech together in 2008. It helped me gain employment at four different companies, at my present job it wasn't necessary since it is a retail position. As I recall, I spent about an hour or so crafting the speech and practicing it in front of a mirror about a dozen times. I wanted it to be perfect every time that I would use it.

On the times I used an elevator speech effectively and got the job I didn't have to wait a day or two for them to call me back. They told me that I was hired before I even got up from my chair to leave the interview office. This just made me feel great and a bit stunned at the same time, actually a bit of a shock. The first time this worked I almost couldn't get out of the chair it was that much of a shock. It was great to send the text message to my wife as I was leaving the building "I got the job, I start on Monday". Right after sending the text message I then update my Facebook status with the same exact message so that everyone could know immediately.

For you to build your elevator speech you need to really delve into what your greatest strengths are in relation to what an employer is looking for. If your strengths and what the employer is looking for doesn't match you just won't be successful I'm sorry to say. Personally I recommend that you have three strengths, and only three for the most effective elevator speech. Preferably these strengths would be ones that very few other prospective candidates for the position will also be offering. Part of why you put together the speech is set yourself apart from the average job seeker.

From my own experience I know that having an elevator speech is really a necessity for any candidate, it really isn't something that you can do without. It's something that should be part of your interview preparation process so that you can be ready at a moments notice. I've even used my elevator speech successfully during one phone interview for a position at Apple. Having that speech ready increased my interview success rate to about 1 job offer out every 7 interviews. That is an amazing number when you think about it, just amazing! It really is an excellent tool to have ready at a moments notice.

Some good sources for samples that you can build into what you specifically need are at:

www.expressionsofexcellence.com/sample_elevator.html

internships.about.com/od/networking/g/elevatorspeech.htm

http://my.jobsdb.com/my/EN/V6HTML/jobseeker/132_care er.html

The words you choose to say something are
just as important as the decision to speak.
Author Unknown

Temp Jobs

"Employment and ennui
are simply incompatible"
Dorothe Deluzy

Temporary jobs through temporary employment agencies can be a good option for many that are seeking a new line of employment. Occasionally, a temp position can become a permanent position which I have had happen twice, once with a moving company and one other at my first call center job. I've also been hired quite a few times for temp positions that would never turn into a permanent hire. Why I chose that option is because I wasn't a big fan of hunting for work, liked working, just not the hunting for a job. An employment agency can be a real time saver, there have been times my entire job hunt was less than a week! They have whole bunch of jobs listed all together in one place and all you have to do is spend a little time talking to a recruiter.

    With temp agencies you need to be prepared to actually go to the local office in most cases. You also need to be prepared to go to multiple employment agencies, don't put your eggs all in one basket waiting for a call from a single agency. As I recall I used to have profiles set up with at two to three employment agencies at a minimum, sometimes as many as eight. My favorite's were Express and SOS, later Volt for more technical employment was added to my favorites list.

    Filling out the online profile may not get you anywhere so be prepared to go the extra step by going in to see an actual person. Every place that you are applying at probably has a stack of applications that they have to go through. Temporary employment agencies are no exception to this rule of the job market. Since it so much easier to submit so many more job applications than it used to be this has become more of an issue. Recruiters, hiring managers and decision makers all get inundated with requests for positions. However, unlike any other place you can go to look for a job, you need to be prepared to talk about all of your employment experience. Temporary employment agencies will be interested in everything that you've done in your work history throughout the years.

Be prepared to try something different, because they are trying to fill a position with a client company the openings available may not match exactly the job you are wanting. You also will go through extensive testing to make sure you can demonstrate what you are saying. If you say you can type you will definitely be taking a typing test. The same goes for Windows, Office software, and anything else that goes with the job.

One thing that is rather common to all employment agencies that I probably should mention is that benefits are not often available through most of the positions that they offer. Also, you may have to wait a bit longer to get benefits if you become hired permanently by the company that you are sent to. This did happen at the call center position I worked at when I became a permanent employee. Still, personally I think having a paycheck is better than not having paycheck in my opinion. Also, eliminating a lot of time hunting for a job was also beneficial to me.

Nothing is predestined:
The obstacles of your past
can become the gateways
that lead to new beginnings.

Here is a fairly short list of temp agencies and their websites. I have mostly focused on nationwide staffing agencies in this list.

Adecco: adeccousa.com

Aerotek: aerotek.com

Apple One: appleone.com

Express Personnel: expresspros.com

Goodwill Staffing: goodwillstaffing.com/

Job Store: jobstorestaffing.com

Kelly Services: kellyservices.us

Manpower: manpower.com

Office Team: officeteam.com

Robert Half: roberthalftechnology.com

SOS Staffing: sosstaffing.com

Staffmark: staffmark.com

Spherion: spherion.com

Volt: volt.com

Time Is Of The Essence

Know how to live the
time that is given you
Dario Fo

In general if you are between jobs and you are looking for a full time job you need to be in the hunt full time. If you are looking for part time employment you need to be devoting less time to the search for a new position. While this is a rather simplistic set of rules to follow it is something that is true. On the other hand if you are looking to change jobs from one you are employed at time is usually on your side. In any job market someone who is employed will be hired over someone who isn't which definitely gives you an edge. You can be choosy which can definitely be of benefit to you in your search for a new opportunity.

When I was in between jobs I had a tendency to devote a lot of time to the job hunt as I was interested in no longer having to hunt for employment. During Monday through Friday I had a tendency to spend about 6-7 hours per day in things pertaining to the job hunt. On Saturday's I would spend less time, about 2 hours that day as there usually weren't too many openings posted. Sunday's I usually spent 2-4 hours total in the job. Altogether, it was roughly about 40 hours per week to find a full time job which is precisely what I was looking for at the time. I was also partially open to part time jobs since I know that they can become full time positions in some cases.

A very old saying that I believe originally came from the Great Depression applies to my outlook regarding this which is "half a loaf of bread is better than no bread". So yes, I was somewhat open to part time employment during some of the job hunts I've been on. It just wasn't a central focus for me to tell you the truth when it came to hunting for a job. Still, almost two years ago from the time I am writing this book I did work part time at a nearby Kmart and then I found an additional part time job in another retail position at a different company. For about two or three months I actually worked at both jobs and I'll admit it was a little tedious at times and it crossed my mind a few times that there might be a scheduling conflict at some point.

About two months into working at both jobs the second company was expanding and was going to open another store. This offered me an opportunity I felt so I went to see the manager rather early in the day to ask to become a full time employee. I was successful with my inquiry, the second job became a full time position so I then quit my part time job at Kmart so that I could devote myself to my new full time position. The point I'm making here is that part time positions can become full time positions. You just need to be open to the possibilities that this can offer you and what you can offer.

Now, back on how I used to utilize the hours in a full time job hunt where I was spending around 40 hours per week searching. This included searching online for job openings, about 2-3 hours Monday through Friday, 1-2 hours on Saturday and Sunday. That time would also include filling out online applications, submitting resumes, taking required tests and double checking all of my online profiles. After that, I felt it was time to get away from the computer for most of the rest of the day. Occasionally I would also spend a few minutes now and then to check my email account to see if I had any responses to any of my applications and then I would be off of the computer again.

Usually I would also do a bit of reading job hunting

books, anywhere from a half an hour per day to an hour. This was to help me be prepared for interview questions and get new ideas for resume changes when it came time for a rewrite. Some of these changes my notes on that I would write down then and I would take a look at a copy of my resume that I had printed at the time. I would then take a few minutes to study my resume, reading through it to make sure that it said what I wanted it to say. Occasionally I would also look at previous resumes also that I was no longer using.

The other main thing that would do during a full time job hunt that paid off better than anything else that I did then is practicing interviews. In particular I would read a couple of the questions and answers in an interview question book that I had as part of my personal employment library. After reading the answer I was able to thoughtfully formulate an answer to the question that was asked. Since I was so much better prepared for an actual interview I was able to be more successful in getting a new job. If I remember right I usually spent about an hour per day studying interview questions alone in our bedroom since it was nice and quiet in there. With raising three teenagers at the time it was very important to have a quiet place to focus on preparing.

Another activity that I normally devoted about a half an hour per day to was thinking of companies that hadn't posted openings. When I thought of one that I hadn't applied to yet I would write it down on a piece of paper. Quite often I would write down a pretty extensive list of prospective employers, sometimes as many as two dozen. This list I would pull out when I was back on the computer after I checked for posted openings at all of the usual places like Monster, Career Builder, etc. About one quarter of my interviews was gained this way by proactively acting.

All work and no play
makes Jack a dull boy
Maria Edgeworth

After I spent all of those hours each day it was time to unwind and relax, usually I was pretty tired after my day. It really was time for a break so that I could continue to make the same effort again the very next day. The whole idea is make your time as productive as possible and to eliminate being out of work for a long time. Personally, finding a job is so much better than looking for a job anytime. You need to use your time effectively and efficiently which will help you to be more proactive in your job hunt and to respond to any calls from employers for interviews. Also, because of your practice each day you'll be more effective when you have an interview.

Thinking Outside The Box

The key to success is to risk
thinking unconventional thoughts.
Convention is the enemy of progress.
If you go down just one corridor of
thought you never get to see what's
in the rooms leading off it.
Trevor Baylis

There are many odd methods of finding jobs out there that are available for you to try if you want though some of the methods may not be all that successful. You just have to want to try something different than everybody else is doing out there. Anybody that tries something out of the ordinary is by very definition a trailblazer and they do have a greater tendency to be successful. Some of these examples I've managed to compile and put together into this chapter are very interesting to read about including a few of my own.

I've seen stories where someone has purchased one of the large ad signs, posted their name and their phone number along with the fact that they were looking for a job. This kind of approach would seem a bit similar to me as the bulk mailer that's sent to every household in a given area. It doesn't seem to me really not very well focused on the people that are actually doing the hiring. While I don't believe that any of these ads were successful if I remember right you have to admit they were trying something a bit different than the average job seeker is out there. I'm not sure that the people washing the CEO's car was successful either but you have to admit that they were really trying to get the job.

A couple of other approaches that was rather interesting

for me to read about was these methods. One the candidate sent in a plate of cookies to the hiring manager. This approach was not successful for them as the cookies did not get them the job. I've also remember reading about the person that had fortune cookies made with their name and phone number printed on the back side of the paper message inside of the cookie. Another had Chinese food containers printed with their name on the outside, they did get a job in marketing for that company but not for the position that they initially applied for. These kind of attempts come more into marketing than anything else I would think. If you want to really change your line of work these kinds of approaches just might be a possibility.

Probably the most interesting story that I've read is about the guy who wrote his entire resume on a sandwich board and walked throughout the entire town. He managed to get quite a few contacts during his journey across the town and if I remember right from one of the stories I read he did manage to get a job out of it. This for me was really thinking outside of the box, shows that he was being very presumptive and that he was also very self-confident. It shows that he really desired to find a job and that he wasn't taking no for an answer, he wasn't going to continue to be unemployed.

Probably the most outside of the box I ever went was applying for a job as a cabinetmaker apprentice. While I knew that I probably wouldn't get the job before I even before I applied because I am over 40 and much older that the average cabinetmaker apprentice usually is. What I was trying to do though was just get the interview, which I did and I felt great about it.

What I did was answer the ad by sending a picture of a bench that I built and is now on our front porch. It looks really great there and frankly it is quite useful for the whole family. I also wrote a small e-mail message that stated that I could cut accurately and straight. Since my customer service background had absolutely nothing to do with the position I didn't send a copy of my resume and I didn't need to. I just did the best I could to demonstrate that I had some of the necessary skills to do the job. This was successful and I was called to set up an interview a couple of days after.

If you're wanting a real change in your life this would be great method for obtaining an apprenticeship based on my results. I also talked to a couple of contractors and they seemed very open to the idea of a picture of a project instead of a resume. These kind of positions you need to be able to demonstrate that you have the skill-set, they aren't entirely interested in what you have done in previous jobs. Handyman positions are also something that is quite possible using this kind of method also. For handyman positions you will need to have some tools ready so that you can show a prospective employer if they ask. While a lot of the handyman positions don't really pay all that well they are steady employment as a rule. Also, these type positions will often include a small apartment and electric because they want you available on site especially at apartment complexes. This can be of real benefit to a lot people and I did it for at two apartment complexes.

Now of course, just like any other job seeker I've made sure that I've had my resume posted on many of the internet job search sites. These have normally been Monster, Career Builder, Indeed and a myriad of others. One day I decided that I wasn't getting quite enough exposure so I posted my resume on Craigslist on their Resume section. Frankly, I can't recommend doing this as it was not successful for me, I received quite a few unusable responses. There weren't any interviews or job offers extended to me and I did receive quite a few advertisements offering to increase my advertising exposure. So, because of this I never tried it again.

One other time that I thought I might discuss happened about twenty years ago. I happened to be in Las Vegas, Nevada walking down the street when I seen an old man putting some furniture out on display in front of the store. I had offered to help him out which he accepted and I worked for about ten minutes putting out all of the furniture. After finishing with putting out the furniture the old man offered me a job which I worked at for about the next six months or so. Because of liability concerns with workman's compensation this might not be as possible these days.

I did not think;
I experimented.
Wilhelm Röentgen

Some of the methods that I have written about in this chapter are pure experimentation, they are so far outside of what would normally be tried. Some of the approaches worked and some of them didn't but you still have to admire the approaches nonetheless that have been tried. If you spend a little time at least thinking of unique job hunting approaches you will probably be more successful at getting interviews. It can help you to think more on your feet and be able change course in an instant when you need to with little or no notice. This is where thinking outside of the box can really pay off in allowing to more effectively adjust to the unexpected that occasionally comes up.

Appearances Matter

Appearances matter and
remember to smile
Nelson Mandela

When you are hunting for a job and meeting employers the way that you dress is extremely important. This tells them a number of things about you some of which you don't know that you are telling them. If you are dressed in torn up blue jeans and a tee shirt you probably aren't making a good impression. This even goes for jobs like construction and similar positions. There are so many people that are looking for a job these days that many employers actually have a lot of candidates applying for the same exact position. Basically you want to look your best when you are meeting decision makers and this is especially during interviews.

So I could look my best in any interview I decided to improve my clothing and have more professional clothing available. Knowing that I needed to set myself apart from the average job seeker I began to collect some suits for the first time in my life. Two of the suits happen to be three piece suits for which I also have color coordinated shirts and ties. While right now they aren't getting any use but they are hanging in my closet ready to put on when I need to in the future. There have been many times that they were necessary in the last couple of years so that I could make a great first impression.

In most of my life I haven't had any need for a suit, in fact I didn't have any professional clothes before 2007. I'll never forget having to look up online how to tie a tie since I didn't know how to do it because I had never needed too. If you don't know how to tie a necktie I recommend checking out www.tie-a-tie.net. The gentleman that set up the site ran into an issue where he had to find out tie his neck tie and couldn't find any information online. If I remember right it was because he needed to know how to do it for an interview. I'm so glad that he set up the site as that's where I actually learned how to do it. For the longest time I kept a link to the site in the browser on our computer after we were no longer homeless.

Most of the jobs I've held you don't usually need a tie for during interviews for house framing, maintenance and moving furniture jobs. In fact those types of jobs you probably still could to show up to an interview in a t-shirt and blue jeans because you need to show you are ready to work immediately. This is especially true during the busy times of the year, usually during the summer. If it isn't the busy time of the year you might want to dress a little better for these types of jobs. Probably I would wear a decent pair of jeans without holes in them and a nice button up shirt. This advice applies to males and females equally.

While you don't absolutely need to wear a three piece suit to every interview I will make some recommendations. You should have a couple of ties, two or three blazers, two or three pairs of slacks and two or three dress shirts. From what I've read the dress shirts should be long sleeved but since I don't like the feel of them on my wrists mine are all short sleeved. While my dress shirts are not long sleeved the sleeves still extend precisely to my elbow. Of additional note the interview clothes do not need to be new, mine had came from Goodwill, Salvation Army, etc. If you do go to such stores make sure there are no stains or tears as there often is, especially check the underarm area. I made the mistake a couple of times of not checking and got very embarrassed during an interview when I finally noticed the stains.

So that you can look your best you'll also need to obtain

an clothing iron and learn how to use it effectively along with an ironing board. Also of note, do not wash the suits in your washing machine as it will cause the seams to tear and the seams to shrink (this is a mistake I made on one blazer). Most Men's suits in particular are made of wool and they do have to be dry cleaned so make sure that you check the label. Since you're primarily wearing the suits for interviews at least they won't need to be dry cleaned all that often.

You'll also want a good pair of dress shoes that goes together well with the suits, slacks and of course some dress socks. The shoes and socks should be color coordinated with the suits that you have. In general, if it's a blue suit then dark blue socks, a medium blue shirt and black shoes should color coordinate together pretty well together. If it's a brown suit then a tan shirt, tan socks and brown shoes should all work well together as a whole. For me, the idea is that by color coordinating everything together it reinforces great first impression that I'm attempting to make. It definitely increases the chances of getting the job I can readily attest to from my very own experience.

Also now that I am thinking about it I would recommend having a brief case or a nice bag for carrying your resumes, cover letters, additional pens, a pad of paper and assorted notes. I guess I would call mine a portfolio bag, it has a lot of pockets and built in dividers and was initially a give away from a drug company. In my closet also there is a very nice brief case that I've only used once or twice before on interviews and those interviews were at banks. For most customer service positions though you really don't need a brief case to carry your resumes and notes.

Both, my portfolio bag and my brief case came from Goodwill or Salvation Army stores just like my suits did. In addition to the other items I also used to carry an interview questions book, that way I could quickly practice a couple of questions before I went in to a place for my interview. "Best Answers to the 201 Most Frequently Asked Interview Questions" by DeLuca is the one I've used and is getting a little dog eared. Of further note is to make sure the interview questions book is not visible at all during an interview. Since I do not drive a car I ended up having to carry everything into the interview with me.

Whenever you have an interview there is one general rule and that is that you only have one opportunity to make a first impression. You probably will not get a second chance in most cases unless you have really good reason. Believe me, it must be a really good excuse especially in this job market and be ready to prove it if need be. Clothing is a big factor in the way a decision maker thinks of you as a candidate, the impression that you are making on them. They will hire a well dressed candidate over one that is not so well dressed every time. Appearances always matter, especially during an interview so you need to make that impression count.

Keeping Track

*The future depends on what
we do in the present.
Mahatma Gandhi*

During a job hunt keeping track of all of your contacts, applications and resume submittals is extremely important. There are a few very good reasons for stating this. One reason is that you can more easily see what approaches is or isn't working very well for you when you look over your results. Another is that you can eliminate applying to the same job over and over again during your job search. I actually had a couple of people that mentioned it when they called me wondering why I was applying so many times for the position. It was a bit embarrassing for me to be told this and it reduces the chances of your being selected for the position.

It really shows that you aren't paying attention to what you're doing. When I look back a few of the decision makers probably came close to laughing when they read in my resume that I was "detail-oriented". It really is no surprise to me now that I wasn't receiving very many responses in those days. When I realized what I was doing after receiving the second call from a decision maker I decided that I needed to make a change in how I was pursuing my job hunt. One of the things I decided to do was keep track of all of my applications and resume submittals.

Thinking about it for a bit I created an Excel spreadsheet on a thumb drive where I could keep track of all of the jobs I applied for. At the time I didn't have home internet service, we were living in a motel after being homeless. Since I still needed to find a job I was using the computers at the unemployment office and at the library. Needless to say in such a situation you need the method you keep track with to be extremely portable. At the library and the unemployment office they had Microsoft Excel and Microsoft Word readily available so it was natural in my mind to keep track using Excel. I was also able to keep a copy of my resume very handy on that thumb drive so I could print it easily.

It made an immediate difference in my whole job hunt from that point forward. At first, when I began to keep track I was rather surprised to learn that I was applying to anywhere from 10-20 jobs per day at times. One printout I still have there are 180 entries in about a month during 2008 and this is after I started to keep good track. It didn't take too long to see the particular positions that I was receiving the most responses from. This allowed me to better focus my efforts to more specific positions as I continued to search for a new job. These days I'm sure I would keeping track in "cloud based" spreadsheet as it is even more portable and I don't have to worry about losing the thumb drive.

At first, I kept track with columns for date, source, job title and company name where possible. Since my job search was mostly by internet quite often the company isn't listed in the postings. Later on, I added pay rate, phone number and interview columns when I began getting more responses from my applications. In the interview column I would put either a Y or N. If it was a Y that would mean that I had received an interview from that company. An N would mean that I had received some kind of correspondence stating that I wouldn't be considered further for the position. Usually, this response was in an email from one of the companies decision makers and sometimes the responses were just generic.

Knowing that I wouldn't be considered any further is actually pretty helpful for me during any job hunt. There were two reasons that I thought it was helpful even if it was a bit of a downer at times. For one, I knew that I was close enough to what they were wanting for the position that an actual person had read my resume or application. For the second reason I could focus my efforts elsewhere and not sit around waiting around for a call that wasn't going to come. This allowed me to be more positive thinking on what I needed to do for other submissions that I was making.

Besides the Excel spreadsheet that I carried on the thumb drive I would also always carry a couple of loose leaves of copier paper with me at all times. This was so that I could make needed notes when I received a call for an interview. These notes included names where possible like the interviewer and the name of who I talked to. Also I made sure that I noted the time of the interview and the address where it was at. After I would look up the address on in an online mapping program I would write down the directions from where I was at or I was going to be. After showing up to the wrong place a couple of times I learned to be very careful in the notes I took.

Since I didn't know precisely when someone would be calling regarding a job I did my best to stay prepared at all times. By making the notes I did it helped me to prepare so much better for the interview. I could refer to the notes I made instead of just relying on my memory alone. This turned out to be especially important at a couple of the call centers where there are multiple doors you could enter the building. Usually, I would double check my notes when I reached the parking lot before I entered the building.

However you do it, you need to keep good track of everything that you can during a job hunt. Your success really does depend on keeping track. You'll be much better prepared for anything unusual that comes up as so often does. About the most unusual thing that I came across was having to have a copy of my high school grade transcript for two different jobs at two companies. If I hadn't wrote it down in my notes I might have easily forgotten that particular request when the time came for the interview.

Quitting Without Notice

*I came very close to quitting my
job for the Bush-Cheney '04 campaign.
I seriously considered packing
up my office and heading home
to Colorado.
Mary Cheney*

As a rule the days are gone where you could quit a job without leaving a two week notice. Yes, I've had a couple of those positions in the past that I didn't leave any notice for. This is not entirely a deal breaker if you do have to mention it during an interview. It really depends on the position that you quit at. Just about any employer will understand if you quit a part time without notice if you got a new full time position. You'll need to be able to explain it though without mentioning anything negative about the position you left.

Normally, most of the positions that I quit without notice at I don't mention therefore it isn't an issue. However, if it was recent and the job you quit at fills a hole in your resume you probably need to mention it. I can think of one position setting appointments for a roofing company. Since I wasn't a very successful appointment setter I didn't make any money. Anyone can understand a person leaving a position without notice where they didn't make anything. My answer when the inevitable question came up was that I wasn't very successful at setting appointments. Usually there was no further questions about the matter during an interview.

How you handle the position you quit at during an interview will determine whether you are hired or not. Anything that invites further questions will probably not be good for your chances. This is where the delicate part really comes in, answering in such a way so it doesn't sound bad and doesn't invite other questions. I don't know of anyone that can do it well, including myself. What will happen is that the interviewer will begin focusing on the position you quit at. They will naturally come to the conclusion you will quit without notice for the new company too.

There was one other job that I had quit without leaving notice that I will mention. For a time I worked at two part time jobs, one of those happened to be at a Kmart. When I was offered full time employment at the other part time job I didn't give notice at Kmart. There was going to be scheduling conflicts I felt so I decided to quit. This is something that I actually mentioned in a couple of interviews. Now if I had mentioned anything about scheduling conflicts during an interview it would be taken negatively. This would have cost me the opportunity in just about every case. You really need to be careful about saying anything that might be taken negatively.

For some jobs it will not be taken too seriously if you have quit without notice. As a rule fast food positions are something that this applies to. Just don't expect them to give you a good reference. I hope that I've indicated well that short term positions aren't too much of a problem. It's the long term positions, ones that are six months or more that are a more serious issue. Any long term position in general needs to be in your resume or written down on an application. Try to avoid bringing it up if at all possible. Since these are the most difficult questions as a rule to answer well you need to be careful here. Think carefully about your answer and rehearse it a lot. There is a lot that will be riding on it for your future.

Resignation Letters

*Never write a letter
while you are angry.*
Chinese Proverb

Congratulations, you have found a new job and you still have a job at present that you are still employed at. This can be a really good thing for you, really you have the best of both worlds when you think about it. I can recommend that you don't want to be burning any bridges just in case something does go wrong. This is where writing resignation letters comes in, especially ones with a two week notice. This allows you to look in the best possible light to both employers which can be a great thing for anyone in the job market today.

In general, any employer that you are listing as a reference you should give a two week notice. There is also the possibility that opens up that if something goes wrong you can retract your letter and continue to work there. Another possibility that opens up is that you can be rehired at that company at some point in the future if need be. This really is the best all around for everyone. There are of course times where you can't leave a two week notice. Some companies want you to start immediately and won't want to wait for two weeks. This is where communicating is very important, you're going to need to talk with someone at the present employer.

More recently I had to create a two week resignation letter because I had found a job with a different employer. This was after a company recruiter had found my profile online and decided to contact me about an opening they had in their call center. Since occasionally recruiters are on the lookout for prospective employees is a good reason why you really do need to keep your online profiles up to date. After they had decided to hire me it turned out there was an issue with my background check and they needed to resubmit it. Because of this they also retracted the job offer that I had just received from them a few days before. Shortly after that I had to in turn request to retract my two week notice from the company that I had been working at.

If I wouldn't have had good communication with my present employer I could have been in serious trouble. I've read of many instances where the person leaving the notice was out of a job, they weren't able to retract their notice. This can add a huge amount of stress to an already stressful situation. I'll admit that in the back of my mind I could easily imagine it happening to me in that instance. Luckily I had great communication with the manager which saved me. It didn't hurt that I was considered a really great employee which is what helped me keep my job.

I've read of many cases in the last couple of years where someone had turned in their two week notice and the employer wouldn't allow them to retract it. This left the employee with very few options, as they now needed a job immediately. Or at least they now needed the job that they have been working at. My personal thoughts are that they didn't have good communication with their boss which ended up costing them. A little better communication probably would have nipped the problem in the bud before it had started. Then again, it might not of but it sure couldn't have hurt them.

Resignation letters are simple things to write in reality. All you need is a sentence or two that states that the last day you'll be working there will be on a date two weeks after the present day. Since it is a type of business correspondence you also need add today's date at the top at the top of the letter. I will recommend that you keep it short and sweet, you don't need to include any of reasons why you are leaving. Keep the letter as brief and diplomatic as possible as this letter will be added to your permanent employment file.

How you treat this situation is very important in just about every case. What I did which probably further helped me in my case is that I requested permission to submit my notice. This went a little beyond common courtesy I'll admit but it was worth it as I still have a job. Never write the letter while you are angry, you'll probably add things to the letter that you really don't want there. These are the things that will cost you by inadvertently burning bridges. Always keep resignation letters professional in nature as your future may depend on it.

I'm not a very good writer,
but I'm an excellent rewriter.
James Michener

Cell Phones

An iPod, a phone, an
internet mobile communicator...
these are NOT three separate devices!
And we are calling it iPhone!
Today Apple is going to reinvent
the phone. And here it is.
Steve Jobs

These amazing devices are now something that are necessary during any job hunt anymore in my opinion. Why you can't do without one is that you need to be reachable at any time just about anywhere. In fact because of extensive job hunting in the past I no longer have a home phone because I didn't find it useful anymore. Thinking about I don't think I'll have one either unless I run a business out of my home. Presently I am using a Blackberry (which I am also writing this book on) but you don't need anything as fancy as that. A simple cell phone on prepaid service will work pretty well also, this is something I did in the past. In most cases you just need to be reachable on the go. Having a message number as the only way to reach you may not be the best option, some employers may not bother to leave a message and go to the next candidate.

I have found over the years that having internet service on your phone to be something very useful. This has made checking my email at a moments notice to be very useful. Also being able to answer recruiter questions on the go has been extremely useful for me at times. It has also made it possible to further research companies and to pull up maps for where I am going to. Having a smart phone makes this even more efficient and easy to do wherever you are at. I've even replied to some employment ads through the phone alone, never having to get on a computer.

Another recommendation I will make is to always have a hands-free set for your cell phone. Because I'm a little hard of hearing at times I personally always use a stereo hands free set. It allows me to hear a caller much better no matter where I am at. Also, no matter where I am its nice to have the ability to listen to music on my phone at. Though I would say that you have to be a bit careful when listening to music while riding a bicycle. In some places though it is illegal so be sure to check your local laws before listening to music and ride your bike. Probably the last thing you want is to get a ticket during a job hunt.

Being reachable at any time is the primary reason to have a cell phone. All the rest of the capabilities that I've mentioned are not, but they do make your life better. Even if they are not necessary the additional capabilities can give you the edge over another candidate. Having an additional edge is not a bad thing to have in any job market. Personally, I like the idea of receiving the call for an interview wherever I am and not have to check for messages at a neighbors house. I've actually had to do that a couple of times many years ago.

On The Web

*Life belongs to the living,
and he who lives must
be prepared for changes.
Johann Wolfgang von Goethe*

When had I originally hit the job market back in 1983 you used to have to do a lot of footwork and hit a lot of doors. You walked to each business that you had identified after you had consulted the phone book. It was a long extensive process where you were lucky to put in two applications per hour, sometimes no more than one or two per day. You also had to get a hold of a copy of the newspaper on Sundays so that you could look through the help wanted ads. In many ways I don't miss that process and all of the time it took though looking in some ways it really was easier.

The internet has changed the job market radically, more radically than anything else has. If you have your on-line profiles set up right, electronic copies of your resumes ready you can apply to 20-30 jobs in less than an hour now. This has contributed to the difficulty in finding employment as there are a lot people with the same capability. You can even have each submission somewhat individualized to each position that you are applying for. This is why I try to always have a customizable generic cover letter and resume at all times. I'm usually prepared to write cover letters from scratch also which is sometimes necessary.

Your resumes should be written in a way that's directly related to the primary field that you're wanting to work in. Then you want to post copies of your resume on several sites, in particular Monster and Careerbuilder and as many others as you can. I will say however that most of my recruiter bites have been from my Monster and Careerbuilder resume and profile postings. A general rule I've followed during job hunts is to run a resume update at least once per month, that way it will get noticed by recruiters more often. If you update it less often you won't get as many recruiting bites. Why this is is because the most recent resumes come when a recruiter runs a search for candidates so keep your resume updated regularly unless you're not looking for a job.

Craigslist is so much different than any other site that you would search for a job at. It's also the one that I've had the most success at when I've been searching for jobs actively, sometimes 70% to 90% of my interviews. Also, my present job and the previous one were both posted on Craigslist. Of course, why it is so different is that it was originally created to make a shopping venue for the average person to both post ads of items they have for sale and for people to find those same posted items. Job listings was something that was added later which I'm glad about. One of the reasons that so many jobs are posted on Craigslist is because job postings are free for employers. Most of the job boards charge which is a major concern these days with profit margins that have been reduced like they are.

For Craigslist submittals I recommend having a copy of your cover letter and resume set up as a non-formatted text file on your computer. Then when you are emailing to the ads e-mail address (highlighted in blue at the top of the ad) you only have to copy the text file (Control + C) and paste it (Control + V) as the body of your e-mail. Then you need to modify the changeable parts of your cover letter like the date and maybe the first sentence. Most of the time (over 90%) you won't have a contact name to put on your cover letter because it's not usually posted in the ads.

Based on various studies that I've seen there will be less employers that will look at what you post on the social network sites. Partially this is because they don't have the time with so many applicants in the job market, partially because they are concerned with a privacy lawsuit at least here in the U.S. Still, I would expect at least some companies will still be checking what comes up when they take a look at your social network profiles. This will continue to be true for the U.S government as a part of their background check process depending on what job you are applying for. Because of this you need to control wherever possible what is posted, especially during a job hunt. Anything negative could be definitely be a factor in the decision of whether or not they will give you an interview.

Linked-In is also another social networking site, one that is actually designed especially for business networking and connections. Though I've had a Linked-In account for a couple of years I can't say that I've had all that much luck with it so far. I've never had a response from posting that I needed a job or finding openings with their job search engine. Then again, as I've stated before I've never been very successful at employment networking functions so my experience may not be entirely helpful.

One other job search site that I should include in this book and I like a lot is Indeed. Indeed is a search engine that pulls in job postings from multiple sources including Monster and Careerbuilder. It's also the only search engine I know of that lists postings from company HR sites like banks and some companies like grocery stores. This can make your employment searching a lot more efficient by saving you a whole bunch of time.

One last site that I will mention is Glassdoor, this is a site I use to research companies now days. Occasionally I've been able to find information that led to really good interview questions to ask. I will also mention that you will see a lot of negative information about the companies, take some of the information you read with a grain of salt. There are a lot of disgruntled employees out there these days.

The internet has really changed things in the job hunt from the way that it used to be. It has expanded your abilities to hunt for a job in ways that was not possible years ago. You just need to focus your hunt very specifically to what you can bring to an employer, what they are looking. This will bring you your absolute greatest chances of success. Make sure that you are reading the ads carefully, I can't stress that clearly enough. A properly focused job hunt online will pay big dividends, I found my present job online and a few others.

The Internet is becoming
the town square for the
global village of tomorrow.
Bill Gates

A list of the sites mentioned in this chapter:

Most newspapers now use Monster instead of their own help wanted ads.
Monster: http://www.monster.com/

Careerbuilder: http://www.careerbuilder.com/

A job search engine that pulls in postings from many sites that is one of the primary one I use.
Indeed: http://www.indeed.com/

Craigslist: http://www.craigslist.org/about/sites/
(This is the international main site)

This site has a lot of company information including pay, benefits, employee reviews, etc. I use it to help me research a company before I apply.
Glassdoor: http://www.glassdoor.com/index.htm

An excellent business networking site that also has a lot of information on companies. You can also find out who the decision makers at a company is through this social network.
LinkedIn: http://www.linkedin.com/

E-Mail Addresses

What's in a name?
That which we call a rose
by any other name
would smell as sweet.
William Shakespeare

Your e-mail address is something that needs to be one that sounds professional. Mine is my entire name minus the last two letters of my last name so that it helps bring my name to mind of recruiters and decision makers. This helps me to sound more professional, helps to draw attention to the rest of my resume. At one time I had an email address that didn't sound too professional. The one I used to have back then was coloradophotopoet@yahoo.com and it really didn't send the message I wanted it to send. It worked well for the poetry that I used to write years ago. After thinking about it for a while I decided to change my e-mail address so that I could sound more professional.

By changing my e-mail address my interview rate did start to go up a bit, I began getting a call every once in a while at least. Since I didn't have everything else covered yet I still wasn't very successful in getting a job I'll admit. Still, it brought me a few more calls for interviews as I began looking more professional to employers. Think about the ads that you see on TV, they are presented a specific way. So are the items in a store while you out shopping, each item is packaged to give the item enclosed the best image in your mind. Your e-mail address is just one small part of the entire package that you are presenting to prospective employer.

Having an e-mail address that is something like

drunkenmonkey@yahoo.com may not exactly present the image of you that you want in an employers mind. This is part of having a professional image to present which helps you to entice an employer to contact you. An unprofessional e-mail address name correlates to being unprofessional in a recruiter or hiring managers mind. You need to take a little time to come up with the best e-mail address that presents you the best.

A good name is better
than precious ointment.
Ecclesiastes 7:1

Cover Letters

For, usually and fitly,
the presence of an introduction
is held to imply that there is
something of consequence and
importance to be introduced.
Arthur Machen

These are like another introduction for you that many employers look for but they don't read in many cases. But since they are part of the consideration process and are looked for by many in HR and by many recruiters they need to be included as a part of your submission. Usually, I will try to call attention to points that were not covered in the resume and I will also call attention to the length of time of total experience. Notice that I've also made it scannable by a person as cover letters are not usually scanned by a computer first. In my opinion you don't need many keywords except ones that an actual person would notice and focus on.

It's in some ways much easier for me to write a cover letter than it is a resume. They are basically a letter, nothing more, that is asking for an interview. It's just that it's best not to directly ask for an interview but to ask for a meeting which I always do in the last paragraph. After the last paragraph I usually also add a presumptive closing, I'm thanking them in advance of meeting them in the interview. This is just using normal psychology to increase the chances of getting called for an interview.

Usually I write most cover letters as a generic letter. There are a couple of sentences that I can easily modify for a given opening. In my case one would be the last word of the first sentence, I can change that word to Monster or Careerbuilder very easily. Also, the additional space after the date is there for a reason. I can add a salutary to specific person or I can get rid of the space altogether. Adding a "To whom it may concern" or "Dear Ma'am or Sir" salutary is considered in bad form these days, it's better to include nothing if you are including one of these.

For those decision makers that actually read cover letters you do need to have perfect spelling and syntax just like in your resume. Because of this you need to take some time writing your basic cover letter. Also, I've made mine to be quickly read and understood in about six seconds which also takes some thought and time.

September 1, 2011

My interest in the above position has prompted me to forward my resume as requested in your advertisement posted on Craigslist.

I am confident that my training and seven years of experience could be effectively applied to the requirements of the position as described. If you would like any additional information, please do not hesitate to contact me.

After reviewing my qualifications I would appreciate a meeting for further discussion on how I may contribute to the organization.

Thanks in advance for your consideration.

Sincerely,
Brian Bigelow

Notice that I have called attention to my total experience in time. I've also called attention to where I found the opening posted at. Since it is actual business correspondence I did date the letter. If I am called to an interview I usually also add the company name and address in block form above the date on a printed copy that I will hand to the interviewer. Below the date I will also add a salutary with the interviewers name when possible also. Notice that I limited the amount of information that I've called attention too. Mostly, I'm wanting to entice someone to look further at my resume, I've simply built an introduction for myself.

While cover letters are not usually something that will not directly get you an interview it is something that is still necessary. If you do not include a cover letter you will reduce your chances for being called. Personally this is not something I ever wanted to do as I really don't like hunting for a job, I like finding a job. A well written cover letter will associate in the readers mind your desire for the position. Make sure your spelling and syntax are perfect just like in your resume. Take a little time and effort to proofread your cover letter, it will be worth the effort.

I was working on the proof of
one of my poems all the morning,
and took out a comma.
In the afternoon I put it back again."
Oscar Wilde

On Writing

I could write a book about it.
I went through a lot of adversity,
but I came back determined
to get my job back and make a
difference. I know I can be here,
and make a difference every night.
Craig Anderson

No matter if you are filling out an application, writing a cover or a resume they all have one thing in common. They all involve writing in some form. In short, the better that you write the better your chances are to receive the call for an interview. This includes making sure all of the spelling is correct and making sure the syntax is correct. While it is a computer that checks your application first it is people that actually will make the decision. You need to make sure the sentences make sense to a human that will be reading.

So that a computer will select your application or resume you need specific keywords as a part of your submittal. There are different keywords for every industry, as a rule no two are alike. It will be different keywords for cashiers then there are for janitors and for salesman. While some similarities will exist for cashiers and salesman as in communication in particular there's a lot of other keywords also. At one time you could find lists of keywords by industry but that is no longer the case. You need to scan ads to try to find the keywords, I've included a few ads here where I've underlined the keywords that I would chose in these actual Craigslist postings.

A healthcare company in Denver is seeking experienced <u>Customer Service Representatives</u>. Prefer candidates with <u>experience</u> or knowledge in <u>Medicare/Medicare</u>. Professional attitude and strong work ethic required. <u>MS Office 2007</u>

Office is looking for part time <u>receptionist</u> for the <u>front desk</u>. Duties include <u>answering phones</u> , greeting clients, promoting our services, cleaning etc. candidates prior <u>experience in retail or sales</u> preferred. We offer competitive pay, good work environment and opportunity for growth

Outside Sales Representative: Long established firm is seeking an <u>Outside Sales Representative</u> for home energy efficient upgrades. Job duties include taking calls from prospective clients, <u>setting appointments</u>, <u>evaluating clients needs</u>, <u>taking detailed measurements</u>, job cost estimating, and following the job through to the end. Base salary plus commission structure, insurance, company vehicle.

Now taking applications for a versatile, reliable, professional individual capable of performing well under pressure. Applicants must be <u>detail orientated</u>, friendly, <u>outgoing</u> and possess professional communication skills. The ability to <u>multi-task</u> is imperative.

We are currently looking for an employee with previous <u>Retail/UPS Store experience</u> for the holiday season. Apply in store only, DO NOT EMAIL YOUR RESUME OR APPLICATION! Could become permanent part time after the holidays.

Join our team in Colorado Springs for <u>retail</u> alcohol sales. Now hiring, FULL time sales associate 35-37 hours. Looking for someone who is dependable, <u>customer service</u> orientated, reliable, friendly, hard working, <u>work well with others*</u> and have ability to lift up to <u>50lbs</u>. Must be 21 years+ and must be able to pass background check and drug screening. TIPS certification a plus.

   *I would note this during an interview in particular.

Cashier Postion

Must be 21
Must pass background check
No DUI's
Must work <u>WEEKENDS & HOLIDAYS</u>
Must have <u>reliable transportation</u>
Experience in <u>retail</u>

With a few exceptions the keywords in these positions are the position name and a few of the attributes required. In the first position MS Office 2007 is also one of note. Knowing how to use specific software is usually a key skill in certain industries, especially call centers. From experience you need to list any experience with MS Office, Internet Explorer and Windows that you have for any call center or secretarial position.

From my resume qualifications section I've highlighted all of the keywords here:

Qualifications: <u>Seven years</u> of <u>customer service</u> with three years of inbound <u>call center</u> experience and presently one year in <u>retail</u> sales.

Note that I've called attention to the length of total employment time, that is a keyword for an individual that is reading my resume. Call center, customer service and retail are all ones that a computer would select and are there for that reason. Notice that retail and customer service is also in quite a few of the job postings above that I've included. Although call center isn't specifically mentioned in any of the job postings that is also one that is really noticed by employers. You have to deal with customers on a daily basis, many of them upset when you work in a call center and employers know this. For the first through the fourth positions I would include any call center experience that you have.

By really reading the ads with a lookout for the keywords it will put you ahead of the game in many cases. The only caution I'll mention is that the keywords that you select must be from your experience. In many cases you'll be asked to prove it in testing though not in every case. Office software knowledge in particular is tested of which I've had many tests for the call center positions that I have worked at. Many positions also will have typing tests also when there is a lot of typing on the job.

Probably the best thing that I could have ever taught myself years ago is to touch type. The year was 1991 and I spent many hours with a typing book and a Smith Corona Galaxy manual typewriter. It was a lot of work but it was worth it for me in the long run. Having learned on the manual typewriter how to touch type helped me get the call center jobs. This also goes to prove that you don't need to go to school to learn some of things that employers are looking for. You just need to know them and be able to prove it.

You writing is one of the first things an recruiter of human resources person will see. Because of this you need to always be at your best in everything you write to get a job. Since it is the first thing they see it actually forms their first opinion of you and of your suitability for the position. After all, they haven't met you yet have they? They are only looking at your submittal and nothing else to see if you are offering what they are looking for.

Resumes

We do not write because we want to;
we write because we have to.
Somerset Maugham

These days writing a resume is actually a necessity for most jobs, even for jobs that didn't require resumes a few years ago like cook and janitorial positions. Since so many prospective employers are now requiring resumes you will need to at least get the basics on how to write a resume effectively. Believe me when I state that the quote I have included above really does apply to the subject of this chapter of the book. It also applies cover letters but they are are covered in another chapter.

Usually a resume is something you need to write that's a bit like an advertisement for you and your skill-set. You are now attempting to write something that will get an employer to want to call you and to meet with you. Even better, after the meeting you they then will offer you a job though that will mainly be if you interview well. There is a process to writing a great resume which I will now begin to cover.

First, you will need to have a definite employment target in mind. In my case it is customer service which really is regularly talking to and interacting with customers. That became a main part of working at the truck stop after I became a cashier there. It took me a little while to figure it out and this is what became my focus in future job hunts. Later on I worked as an inbound customer service representative in call centers and now I'm working in commissioned sales in a retail store. Whether it's sales or call center work it's still customer service which is the focus that I chose for my life beginning late in 2006. For you the focus will probably be something completely different than something that I have chosen or will choose.

Second, you need to focus on the value that you will be bringing to a new employer. In my case it is a lot of experience in communicating with customers and the various skills that relate to customer service. Presumably any employer would gather from my resume that I will be bringing that experience and value to them and that it would be a benefit their company for that's the way I attempted to write my resumes. Regardless of who you are or what you do you need to be able to do that also because you need to demonstrate the value you are bringing.

Third, now you need to build both of the first two into one single document. Together, when you look at my newer customer service resume which is the first one you'll come to in that chapter you'll be able to see that I have built both of those together into that same document.

It takes quite a while to write a great resume, you need to write a decent rough draft and then edit it many times and I do mean many times. You won't get a great resume written immediately, no one does. As I recall it took me several hours to get my first resume and to tell you the truth it wasn't very good. After several rewrites though it began to look a bit better but it still wasn't what I needed as I wasn't getting very many calls. I think my response rate was in the neighborhood of one out about every three hundred resumes sent out. It actually took me a year or two before I started to write much more effective resumes.

To get your rough draft you will need to make a list of the various tasks you have done and the various skill-sets used in your different jobs. These are the things that you will be highlighting in your resume. How I started was to write down a list of the various tasks that I done and skills that I built at the truck stop. Then I did some research on who was hiring, also did some thinking about what I wanted to do with my life from that point forward. By doing that I was able to begin targeting my resume to more specific positions.

Also, I did some research on what employers was looking for in customer service representatives. As I remember I began going through the want ads posted on-line, I was looking for keywords that were in the ads. These I began interspersing throughout my resume and began creating the entries around the keywords. This way I knew that my resume would come up when they were looking for a new employee. Whenever you write a resume it needs to be written with keywords, the more the better. Why this is is because a computer probably will read your resume before an actual person does especially when you are submitting resumes electronically. At the same time you need to write your resume for a person to read and understand. This is not something that is easy to do at first as I stated a little earlier.

You no longer need an objective section; while it used to be normal and customary on resumes it no longer is. It is also something you will see in most older resume writing books and you will see it in my older resume. Part of why that went out was the deluge of resumes that began being sent out starting in 2007, employers should be able to infer your compatibility from the qualifications section. Also, a computer will be the first one scanning your resume for keywords of course. If you haven't included the appropriate keywords you will not be called, that is the simple truth of the matter.

When writing a resume I recommend adding as many keywords as you can in the qualifications chapter which should be your first section. A qualifications section highlights the rest of the resume that you are writing and will be submitting. From my research that I've conducted there are a number of HR people that will go no farther than the qualifications chapter of any resume. Because of this you need to really write this section well as it is your introduction, also for those HR people and recruiters that will read farther you need to write the rest just as well. Just remember, don't duplicate anything in the rest of the entries that you have written in your qualifications chapter.

Any time you can truthfully state that you were the only one to do something that applies to the job you are applying for you it needs to be added it in your entries. Any promotions also need to be noted, each preferably highlighted with a bullet point as you want these noticed. Also, if you have a security clearance that was granted by any government agency make sure you note that too under the appropriate job entry like I have on the USPS help desk.

Notice in each of the resumes I've included that I'm calling attention to specific abilities which are based on the jobs that I'm searching for. The first one which is more recent is written for customer service positions, the second one which is older is for IT help desk positions and also I would submit it for cell phone store and electronic sales positions. While it was successful for IT help desk position consideration and to get interviews I will admit that resume was not successful in getting interviews for the other positions that I had been applying for. Probably this is because it is so much more technically oriented than what they are looking for.

Sometimes reading other peoples resumes has been helpful to me when I've been re-writing my own which is why I'm including two of mine in this book so that you have an actual example. Note that immediately at the beginning of the qualifications chapter I've included the length of total experience in customer service. Many employers do consider length of time an important consideration in the decision whether to interview you or not so I've called attention to it right at the beginning. From my research this really becomes a decision factor when you have at least three years of experience in a given field.

In both cases these resumes are very similar, but they are both at the same time calling attention to different aspects of my experience. I've attempted to make both resumes what is called scannable, that someone can read through them in less than a minute and understand what I'm trying to get across to them. They are also written very specifically with as many appropriate keywords as possible so that a computer will scan them and select them. Without the computer selecting them it won't get to a person for any consideration in the process and call for an interview.

Here is my present resume:

Qualifications: Seven years of customer service with three years of inbound call center experience and presently one year in retail sales.

Demonstrating these skills and abilities consistently:
* Efficient multitasking ability
* Excellent communication skills
* Advanced customer service skills
* Extensive computer skills

Experience:
4/10-present Pleasures   Colorado Springs, CO
Retail Clerk – Maintaining excellent customer relations to develop increased customer loyalty. Conducting transactions accurately wile using effective active-listening skills. Assisted in opening the new Platte Avenue location for the company.

Performing accurate and thorough inventories during weekly store product deliveries.

8/09-2/10 AAA Member Services Colorado Springs, CO
Customer Support Professional – Accurately processed changes for Northern California members on existing auto policies. Effectively used active-listening skills to ensure accuracy on all changes.

12/08-6/09 Comcast Colorado Springs, CO
Customer Service Representative – Excelled at assisting customers in resolving issues with billing, internet and television services.

10/07-8/08 Hewlett Packard Colorado Springs, CO
Help Desk Agent – Supported U.S. Postal service employees with Microsoft Word, Excel, Outlook and Windows XP issues in a call center environment.
* Top Agent Award in May 2008
* Sensitive Security Clearance

1/07-10/07 ICT Group Colorado Springs, CO
Customer Service Representative – Analyzed needs to help Virgin Mobile customers find solutions to cell phone service and billing issues.
* One of the few temporary employees to be hired permanent

11/02-11/05 Tomahawk Truck Stop Fountain, CO
Janitor, Inventory, Cashier – Maintained store cleanliness when originally hired then took on additional responsibilities with store order deliveries and inventories. Performed transactions and cash drawer balancing accurately and efficiently once promoted to cashier.

* Only janitorial employee ever promoted to cashier

Education
12/05-6/06   Kaplan University online
20 credits, Paralegal   President's List Honors

This resume is from about December 2009 that was posted on Dice:

Objective Customer Service

Qualifications
Six years of outstanding customer service with three years of inbound call center experience. Proven ability to apply problem-solving skills to identify root causes and determine appropriate actions
* Efficient multitasking ability
* Excellent communication skills
* Highly developed organizational skills

Experience
8/09-present   AAA Member Services Colorado Springs, CO
Customer Support Professional-Successfully communicating with members while correctly processing insurance policy changes. Effectively use active-listening skills to strengthen member retention and increase satisfaction.

12/08-6/09   Comcast   Colorado Springs, CO
Customer Service Representative-Excelled at assisting customers resolve issues with billing, internet, telephone and television services.

10/07-8/08   Hewlett Packard   Colorado Springs, CO
Help Desk Agent - Supported U.S. postal service employees with Microsoft Word, Excel, Outlook and Windows XP issues in a call center environment.
* Top Agent Award in May 2008
* Sensitive Security Clearance

1/07-10/07   ICT Group   Colorado Springs, CO
Customer Service Representative - Analyzed needs and helped Virgin Mobile customers find solutions to cell phone service and billing issues.
* One of the few temporary employees to become permanent

11/06-1/07   Arinc   Colorado Springs, CO
Auditor - End of year inventory audit that was created with Microsoft Excel.

6/06-11/06   Microsoft and Skype Fountain, CO
Beta Tester - Tested beta versions of Microsoft Office 2007 and Skype.

11/02-11/05   Tomahawk Truck Stop   Fountain, CO
Janitor, Inventory, Cashier - Found ways to increase accuracy and improve efficiency.
* Only janitorial employee to be promoted to cashier

Education
12/05-6/06   Kaplan University
20 credits, Paralegal   President's List Honors

94-95   NRI Schools
Certificate, Computer Repair   Achieved high honors

Throughout both resumes you'll notice bullet points, these are for accomplishments that I want attention called to. This especially applies if the accomplishment was a rare one like being the only one to do something. In my case it happened to be my promotion to cashier at the truck stop. Having checked again I'm still the only one to do that ever. As a rule, the more accomplishments you have listed the better off you are. Just make sure the accomplishments apply to the new position you are applying to.

Another accomplishment to call attention to with a bullet is if you were recognized as employee of the month at any time. In my case it was the top agent award that I received at the USPS help desk. This was their equivelant to employee of the month for the contractor that I actually worked for. While I didn't actually work directly for Hewlett Packard I did work at their facilty. Most employers wouldn't have heard of Volt Services they have heard of Hewlett Packard.

You also do not have to list the exact job titles that you've held. In some cases I've forgotten exactly what the job titles actually were. What I've done is made them the most similar to both describe the position and what anyone would understand when they read my resume. Your resume is an important document that must be written effectively. Do not get overly wordy at any time, if a word does not need to be there then remove it when you edit.

A successful resume is one that gets you calls for interviews. If you are not getting calls for interviews you need to rewrite it. This one document must be written and rewritten with that in mind always. With a properly written resume you will never again have to be out of work for very long. This is a fact and has helped me to find many jobs in the last few years. It will help you out also so that you can be successful in getting the job you want.

Getting To The Interview

The bicycle is a curious vehicle.
Its passenger is its engine.
John Howard

Just like anything else during a job search you need to be prepared ahead of time for how you are going to get to the interview. What I've done in the past is to map out my route to the interview usually with an online mapping database like Google maps. This is because I always want to make sure I get to the interview on time, preferably ahead of time. One of the features of Google maps that I like is that it shows how long it takes to get from beginning to end of the trip to the interview. Presently, to double check I would pull up a last minute map of the area where the interview is at on my phone.

Usually being on time is considered being about 10 minutes ahead of the time the interview is set for. If there any papers to fill out then you need to probably add another 5 minutes ahead. Any earlier than this in the office itself you will be overly early, this will be something that won't be considered well. Also, I like to get to the parking lot about 5 minutes before I enter the office, that way I can prepare somewhat before. This includes a few moments of meditation. I'll also mention that showing up to the interview a few minutes late will probably not be good for your chances. They will probably still give you the interview but they probably won't hire you.

A note I'll make is if you ride a bicycle to the interview you might not want to let the interviewer know. This is usually considered an issue by most employers as they will think that you might not make it to work on time. For convenience stores and smaller retail establishments you probably don't want them seeing your bike if at all possible either. If you ride a bicycle everywhere, like I do, then you might want to call attention to your perfect attendance at previous positions. In my case I have had perfect attendance at every job I have held, this is where I direct the interviewers attention.

Being on time will reflect upon how the interviewer perceives how you will do in the position when it comes to attendance. This is why you can't be late! If you are overly early and they know it they will think that you have too much time on your hands. They will think that you will also sit around if they hire you and not work, this is not a good thing. As a rule, I began stopping a couple of blocks away from the interview site to prepare myself a bit further. Taking a few minutes I would meditate to clear my mind and to get rid of the jitters. Since I'm one of those naturally nervous people jitters are a real issue for me.

To be on time to an interview is something that requires preparation in all cases. Make sure you know where you are going, map it out no matter what. It doesn't matter what kind of map, it can be a map out of the phone book even. This is how I used to map out everything years ago, I'll still sometimes look at a phone book map for whatever reason. Personally technology has made mapping out your trip to the interview so much easier. So use the tools that are widely available so that you can look your best.

Interviews

At least for me personally,
I've always tried to do a
really good job every day,
with each interview, and
treat each interview seriously,
and make the person I'm
speaking with feel comfortable,
hopefully make it an ideal experience.
Katie Couric

You've now managed to get an interview set up successfully for a new job at a new company. You have also spent many hours preparing for the questions that you know you will be asked during the interview. On a little piece of paper you also have a set of questions ready that you will be asking your interviewer at the end of the meeting. Copies of your resume and cover letter are ready in the folder that you are carrying in with you. Adding to the feeling of confidence is the fact that you have researched the company and the position that you are about to interview for.

Getting to the parking lot 20 minutes before the time of your interview you take a few moments to comb your hair, straighten your suit and your tie a bit. You are now as ready as you can possibly be so you walk across the parking lot to the building on the way to the office inside. Someone is approaching the door at the same time so you wait a few moments to open the door for them. After all, the person you are opening the door for now just might be the person who is going to be interviewing you shortly. Of course it might not be your interviewer but if the right person happens to seen you being courteous to others their impression of you will probably be pretty favorable which really isn't a bad thing. This will especially be true at convenience stores.

Two of the greatest assets that you can have during a job hunt is being as prepared as possible and common courtesy. Preparation is important so that you have just about everything covered though there will always be some unexpected things that will come up. The more prepared you are the better you will be able to deal with the unexpected when it happens. Courtesy is important because every company is looking for ways to retain customers, gain new ones and for coworkers to get along with each other. By opening the door for someone you are showing those particular tendencies.

So that you can prepare effectively for the interview I recommend a technique that I've used that helped me a lot. Interview yourself in front of a mirror so that you can see yourself, your body language and your mannerisms. Listen carefully to yourself as you speak so that you can sound more professional at the actual interview. This is an actual method that I've read about actors using and I've recommended in my job hunt Facebook group.

I remember watching the Today Show one morning a few years ago and they were talking about body language on the show. How you sit, how you move and hold your hands, how you stand speaks volumes about you and many times you don't realize it. At the time I had the tendency to slouch which didn't make me look very good during an interview and I didn't know why that I wasn't getting any of the jobs that I was interviewing for. Many times also I couldn't look at the interviewer direct and make any eye contact.

How I discovered what I was doing wrong was right after the show I went into the bedroom and sat on the bed in front of the mirror. Then I began to interview myself using some of the questions from an interview question book. It didn't take long to observe what I was doing, when I began to see it in the mirror. This is something that I decided was definitely going to change immediately and for good. Every day for several days I interviewed myself in front of that mirror watching how I was acting, making sure that I was making eye contact with my reflection. When you think about it during an interview you use acting skills to be able to help you to get the job. Just don't go too far outside of what you would normally do or how you would normally act. This will be immediately apparent after start working if you have been successful at the interview you are now at.

You have now entered the door and you meet the person at the desk and let them know that you are there. Now you take a seat in the room to wait and prepare your mind for what you are about to do. At this point I usually do a little meditation, clearing my mind to be better prepared for the meeting. Usually I'll set my resume portfolio on my lap with my hands on top of it. Then I close my eyes and let my mind empty for a minute or two. Since I usually carry multiple versions of my resume now is the time I take to open my portfolio and double check which one I will give the interviewer.

Now, the interviewer comes out to meet you and guide me to the room where they are conducting the interview with you. They greet you and extend their hand for a handshake. This handshake can't be overly firm like you're breaking their hand, it can't be too limp, it must be just right. An image of the three bears porridge story does come to mind when I think of this. Since I knew how much is riding on this handshake because of the impression it makes I practiced on everyone that I met for several weeks even at the local convenience store, the bank and anywhere else that I would meet someone. I wanted my handshake to be just right.

Both of you are now in the room where the interview is taking place. Now is your chance to really shine by having many examples of your answers in action which are done with short stories. These stories must demonstrate the qualities that the interviewer is wanting to hear. Here are a few common interview questions that I've received many times at various interviews.

"Tell me about yourself." There are no really right or wrong answers with this one. You need a general answer for this one since it is usually used as a warm up. "Describe the best job you've ever had." This question is on the edge of difficult, you need to pick the job you've worked at that is most similar to the one you're interviewing for. Naming a job too dissimilar to the one you're interviewing for will cost you the opportunity. "What is your greatest accomplishment?" Have an accomplishment ready for this question, I had it asked in about half of all of the interviews that I've been in.

"What is your biggest/greatest weakness?" I'll admit I've never had a good answer for this but this answer is not a deal breaker. Two of the jobs that I've worked at during the interview I had been asked this question. "What do you know about our organization/business?" About half of all interviews I've been on this question has been asked. My usual answer is "what I know about the business is what I was seeing at the company website." Usually I'll try to have at least one particular thing that stands out from going to the website. "Where do you see yourself in five years?" This one could be dangerous to your candidacy depending on how you answer it. It's probably not a good idea to answer that you'll be running the company which I made the mistake of doing long ago.

"How did/do you get along with your coworkers?" My

usual answer is "I always get along with everyone" which is true as it goes along with customer service. If you had an altercation with an employee you may not want to mention it now. "How long will you stay with us?" This question usually denotes that they are looking for a long term employee, one that will be working there at least two years. "Can you work overtime?" If you can't you might want to let them know now just don't expect to get the job.

Notice that all of these questions are open ended, they are meant to get you to talking. Since they are intending to get you talking, indulge them. Demonstrate verbally that you are the right one for the job, that you are the one they are looking for. "Do you have any questions for me?" You need to have two to three questions ready to ask the interviewer, no more, no less. Any more than three questions will cost you the opportunity having tested it in a number of interviews. If you don't have any questions to ask you have just demonstrated that you aren't all that interested in the job which means that you won't get the job.

My favorite and most successful questions are these. "What do you like best about working here?" This nice open ended question gets the interviewer talking and tells them that you are really interested in becoming a part of the organization. "How long have you been working here?" A short question that evokes a short answer, with this answer I can tell how much they like working at that company. "How do you measure employee performance?" This question shows that I'm thinking of being a part of the organization and that I'm thinking long term.

You're now at the end of the interview, this is when I usually interjected with my short closing statement/elevator speech reiterating what I felt was my best three qualities. Also I would state that I looked forward to working there a long time, be a part of the team and that I was looking forward to their call. Now is the time to leave the room gracefully and it's also time to get home and out of the suit. You can relax now, the worst is over for now.

Phone Interviews

*But in this case, he had my cell phone
and my phone was ringing and I had
just come back from Australia on the
plane and I thought it was my mum
and it was Woody Allen just checking
to see if I wanted to be in his movie.*
Radha Mitchell

Phone interviews are much like a personal interviews in so
many ways and yet so much different in some other very
important ways. The main difference is that you can receive a
call at any time to be interviewed wherever you are. This is one
of the main reasons that I recommend that you need a cell
phone during a job hunt. Also quite often a short phone
interviews are conducted to help someone decide whether to
give you an in person meeting or not as a part of the pre-
screening process. Since there are so many candidates
applying for jobs these days pre-screenings have become more
important in the decision process.

From personal experience phone interviews are quite
commonly not as formal as in person interviews though there
are exceptions to this. Part of what gives the phone interview a
less formal feeling is the fact that you don't have to dress up.
You could easily interview while wearing your sleep wear
which I had happen a couple of times. Yet because of
everything that is riding on the call you need to be just as
prepared as you would be for personal interviews. Don't let
yourself get stressed out over the phone interview because
you'll do so much better and be much more successful.

I don't think I'll ever forget one phone interview for a

help desk position with Apple that I had while riding my bicycle down town one day. As I recall I was riding my bicycle in what was a lot of traffic and was stopped at the light when the call came in. Luckily at the time I had a stereo hands-free set attached to my cell phone or I couldn't have heard the caller. After the light turned green I rode to the next block I pulled up to the curb, parked my bike at one of the trees and stood in front of a bagel shop so I could continue the interview. I'll admit it was a little bit difficult for me to answer the questions and ride my bicycle.

This interview was not a short one, as I recall it took about 45 minutes since it was a complete interview and it was one of the exceptions that happens during a job hunt. This shows that you need to be ready for anything to happen at any time. Being able to be reached at any time probably is the most important. I've heard of business owners that couldn't reach someone directly and went to the next name on their list. It may be unfortunate but the business owner has a need that must be filled and many don't feel that they can wait.

Phone interviews are something that are a major part of the process that is used these days. You can make it through any phone interview just like you can a personal interview. Preparation is the key every time and in every instance. Your next opportunity could very well be one phone call away!

More Links

*One of the Internet's strengths is its
ability to help consumers find the right
needle in a digital haystack of data.
Jared Sandberg*

These are more links that will help you a lot during your job
hunt. First I will start with an online word processor and
spreadsheets. While it does a really good job with resumes in
the word processor it doesn't quite have all of the features that
MS Word or OpenOffice has but it you can pull up your
document just about anywhere. You can upload your Word
resume too so that you can have it available as long as there is
internet access. For Google Docs and Maps you will need to
have a Gmail account. I will note that you need to access
Google Docs from a computer, you cannot edit your docs from
a phone web browser.

Google Docs: https://docs.google.com/#home

While computers as a rule have spell and syntax checks it's still
a good idea to have a dictionary and thesaurus available.

Merriam-Webster: http://www.merriam-webster.com/

To find where you are going and how to get there. Google
maps has a really nice routing feature for cars, walking,
bicycles and bus.

Google Maps: http://maps.google.com/

Having all of your web links on one site can be very useful during a job hunt especially when you are using multiple computers for your job hunt.

Delicious: http://delicious.com/

Google Bookmarks: https://www.google.com/bookmarks/ Some really good job hunt information is available at these sites.

About: http://jobsearch.about.com/

Blue Sky Resumes: http://www.blueskyresumes.com/

Career One Stop: http://www.careeronestop.org/

Job-hunt: http://www.job-hunt.org/

Tim's Strategy: http://timsstrategy.com/

These are job boards not listed otherwise in this book. Mostly they are search engines pulling in jobs from multiple sources. While you can set up accounts at all of them I don't recommend it and I've had accounts at most of them. Check them all out and pick a couple of them that you like and will mostly use.

America's Job Exchange: http://www.americasjobexchange.com/

Bank Jobs: http://www.bankjobs.com/

Dice: http://www.dice.com/

I Hire Banking: http://www.ihirebanking.com/

Job: http://www.job.com/

Job Central: http://www.jobcentral.com/

Job Spider: http://www.jobspider.com/

Juju: http://www.job-search-engine.com/

Just Jobs: http://justjobs.com/

Linkup: http://www.linkup.com/

Nation Job: http://www.nationjob.com/

Simply Hired: http://www.simplyhired.com/

Snag A Job: http://www.snagajob.com/

The Ladders: https://www.theladders.com/

This a search engine for Twitter.
Twit Job Search: http://www.twitjobsearch.com/

Worktree: http://www.worktree.com/

For Government employment, listings from just about every branch of the government is found here.
USA Jobs: http://www.usajobs.gov/

On Smoking

Acting for me is not a bad habit
like smoking that I must
make an effort to quit.
I love acting; I love directing.
Joan Chen

Unless your interview is with a tobacco manufacturer you probably don't want to be seen smoking. In fact even interviews at most tobacconists I wouldn't recommend smoking anywhere within view. Don't let a pack of cigarettes be visible during an interview either, they need to be hidden out of site. Anymore cigarettes are seen as a negative during an interview and by many companies, some companies now won't hire you either if you smoke and some even test for nicotine. One company that I've known about a long time that tests for nicotine makes concrete pieces for landscaping. From the more recent studies I've seen public perception in general is negative regarding smoking and smokers.

Yes, I do happen to have this habit myself and have learned the way that the wind is blowing. In general the rule I follow is that if I am within a block from where my interview is I don't smoke. There are a couple of bank interviews where I didn't get the job because the interviewer had seen me smoking across the street. At the time I was attempting to get a job as a teller, I didn't realize that my interviewer had seen me across the street. Of course, my age and the fact that I rode the bus probably also contributed to her decision not to hire me. As a rule though banks are exceedingly negative on smoking so don't let them see you smoke.

Make sure you brush your teeth within about an hour

before your interview. You don't want to smoke heavily either before you see the interviewer. Make sure that any cigarette you smoke is downwind from you, you don't want to see the interviewer when you smell of cigarette smoke. You can be a smoker and still get a job you just have to be careful how you do it during the job hunt.

In Closing

Final thoughts are
so, you know, final.
Let's call them closing words.
Craig Armstrong

I think the original idea for this book came to me was when I was sitting at bus stop after work one day in Spring 2009. It has also cropped up a few times after that occasionally since then. So, this book has actually been on my mind for quite a while but I never acted on actually writing anything. It was something where I was thinking that I might do it some time. Well, finally I began putting everything together after running the group almost a year on Facebook that this book is named for. I realized that I had accumulated a lot of information and I wanted to put it all together in one place for the group and for my two Sons.

Hopefully you got a lot out of this book, it has been quite a project for me to write. I've had to learn many things having to do with page formatting, software, how to submit the manuscript and so much more. Some of that same drive that helped me to get a job definitely helped me to write this book. All in all I've really enjoyed putting it all together and sharing all of my experiences with you. Please accept my appreciation for you my dear reader for reading this book and sharing a small part of my life. I'll close with this last quote:

When you arrive at a
fork in the road, take it.
Yogi Berra

Notes

Notes

Notes

www.ingramcontent.com/pod-product-compliance
Lightning Source LLC
Chambersburg PA
CBHW051334170526
45166CB00002B/809